# READY, SET, DRAW!
# SUPERHEROES

## AILIN CHAMBERS

W
FRANKLIN WATTS
LONDON•SYDNEY

First published in 2015 by Franklin Watts

Franklin Watts
338 Euston Road
London
NW1 3BH

Franklin Watts Australia
Level 17/207 Kent Street, Sydney, NSW 2000

Produced by Arcturus Publishing Limited,
26/27 Bickels Yard, 151–153 Bermondsey Street, London SE1 3HA

Editors: Samantha Hilton, Kate Overy and Joe Harris
Illustrations: Dynamo Limited
Design concept: Keith Williams
Design: Dynamo Limited and Notion Design
Cover design: Ian Winton

A CIP catalogue record for this book is available
from the British Library.

Dewey Decimal Classification Number 743.4
ISBN 978 1 4451 4190 9

Printed in China

SL003595UK

Supplier 03.. Date 1214, Print run 3888

# CONTENTS

# GRAB THESE!

**Are you ready to create some amazing pictures? Wait a minute! Before you begin drawing, you will need a few important pieces of equipment.**

### PENS AND PENCILS

You can use a variety of drawing tools including pens, chalks, pencils and paints. But to begin with use an ordinary HB pencil.

### PAPER

Use a clean sheet of paper for your final drawings. Scrap paper is useful and cheap for your practice work.

### ERASERS

Everyone makes mistakes! That's why every artist has a good eraser. When you rub out a mistake, do it gently. Scrubbing hard at your paper will ruin your drawing and possibly even rip it.

## RULER

Always use a ruler to draw straight lines.

## COMPASS

You can use a compass to draw a perfect circle. However, some people find this tricky. Try drawing round a coin, bottle top or any other small, round item you can find.

## INK PENS

The drawings in this book have been finished with an ink line to make them sharper and cleaner. You can get the same effect by using a ballpoint or felt-tip pen.

## PAINT

Adding colour to your drawing brings it to life. You can use felt-tip pens, coloured pencils or water-based paints such as poster paints, which are easy to clean.

# GETTING STARTED

In this book we use a simple two-colour system to show you how to draw a picture. Just remember: new lines are blue lines!

## STARTING WITH STEP 1

The first lines you will draw are very simple shapes. They will be shown in blue, like this. You should draw them with a normal HB pencil.

## ADDING MORE DETAIL

As you move on to the next step, the lines you have already drawn will be shown in black. The new lines for that stage will appear in blue.

## FINISHING YOUR PICTURE

When you reach the final stage you will see the image in full colour with a black ink line. Inking a picture means tracing the main lines with a black pen. After the ink dries, use your eraser to remove all the pencil lines before adding your colour.

The method shown on the left is perfect if you want to draw a character in the same pose every time. But what if you want to draw the same character in lots of different poses?

### STEP 1: START WITH A STICKMAN

Place a piece of paper over a character you like and trace it as a stickman. How big or long are the arms, legs, head and body?

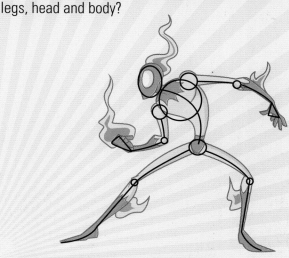

### STEP 2: STRIKE A POSE!

Draw a new stickman in a different position, making sure that the arms, legs, head and body are exactly the same size as in your first traced picture.

### STEP 3: ACTION!

Now you can flesh out your character in the new pose. Once you are happy with what you have drawn in pencil, add inks and colours.

# THE FIREFLY

**The Firefly is a bug-eyed hero with amazing fire powers. Red-hot living flames leap out from his body to capture criminals.**

### STEP 1

First, copy these shapes to create his head, torso and superhero underwear.

### STEP 2

Next, add these long, thin shapes for his long arms and thighs.

### STEP 3

Give your superhero a pointy chin, clenched fists and curved lower legs.

### STEP 4

Now it is time to add those flames. You can also draw bulging arm muscles on his upper arms. Add two lines to join his torso and underwear.

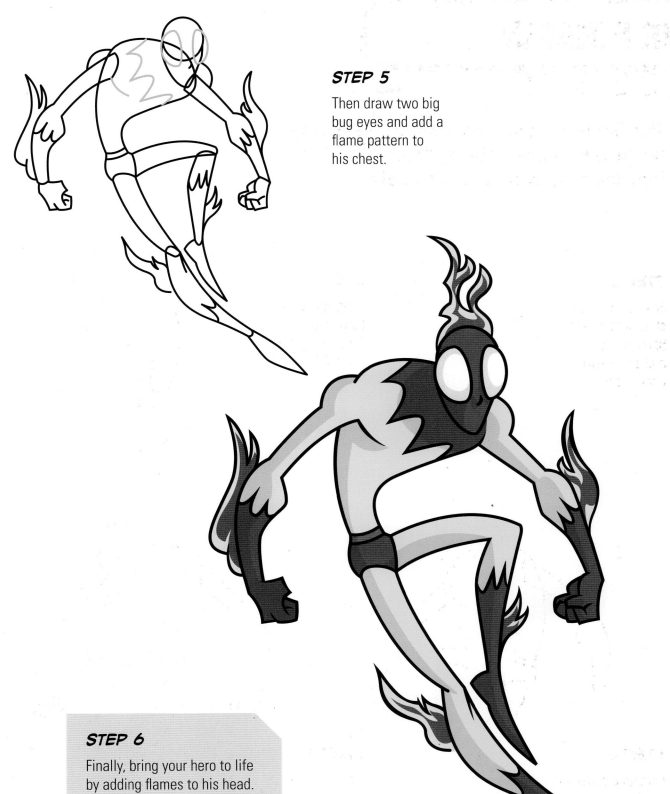

**STEP 5**

Then draw two big
bug eyes and add a
flame pattern to
his chest.

**STEP 6**

Finally, bring your hero to life
by adding flames to his head.
Use bright colours such as
yellow and red for his body.

# MISS MIRACLE

With her long, flowing cape, Miss Miracle is ready to fly into action. She keeps her true identity a secret with her green eye mask.

## STEP 1

Begin by drawing Miss Miracle's head, body and pelvis.

## STEP 2

Draw her arms and thighs next.

## STEP 3

Add an ear and a pointed chin to give her a heart-shaped face. Then add hands and lower legs.

## STEP 4

Next draw her neck, upper lip, belt and feet. Give her long hair and an eye mask.

## STEP 5

Now it's time to add the details to her face and clothes. Don't forget her flowing cape.

## STEP 6

Enjoy colouring Miss Miracle. Pick out the details on her clothes in a different shade to make them stand out.

# WHIZZ-KID

**You don't have to be a grown-up to be a superhero. Whizz-Kid is a teenager who can move with lightning speed.**

### STEP 1

First, draw a peanut shape for Whizz-Kid's torso, then a circle for her head.

### STEP 2

Next, add carrot shapes for her upper arms and thighs.

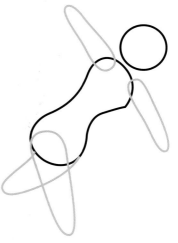

### STEP 3

Add her chin and ear. Then draw her lower arms and legs to make it look as if she is racing to the rescue.

### STEP 4

Draw her feet, hands, neck, hair and eyes. Then add other details to her outfit as shown here.

### STEP 5

Finish sketching her face, eye mask and hair. Add the sharp, jagged lines to her costume.

### STEP 6

Don't forget the lines and puffs of smoke to show that she is zooming into action. Then colour her however you like.

## SUPER TIP!

**Puffs of smoke show sudden movement. They are easy to draw:**

- In pencil, draw circles of different sizes. Overlap them until you have the shape and size of puff you want.

- Ink round the edge of the shape. Then rub out the inner parts to finish your puff of smoke.

# DOC PARADOX

**This evil scientist spends all day in his laboratory thinking of nasty ways to take over the world. His latest invention, the Impossi-tron, might help him do just that!**

### STEP 1

Start by drawing the Doc's lab coat.

### STEP 2

Next, add a big, round head, sleeves and trousers.

### STEP 3

Now draw his ear and big chin, hands and feet.

### STEP 4

Enjoy drawing that crazy hair. Then add his neck, the front of his lab coat and the bottom of the Impossi-tron.

## STEP 5

Next, draw the Doc's mad, googly eyes and face. Add the shirt details and the rest of the Impossi-tron.

## STEP 6

Draw energy waves coming from the top of the Impossi-tron. Then colour the Doc in. You could add a faint scar on his head.

15

# CAPTAIN FANTASTIC

**Captain Fantastic has everything a superhero needs. He's got super-strength, super-speed, super-good looks and a really super hairstyle.**

## STEP 1

First, draw the Captain's wide body and head. Then add a vertical line to find the centre of his head and neck. This will help you get everything in the right place.

## STEP 2

Draw two more lines from the top of his head to make a triangle. Then, add the bulging arms, legs and feet.

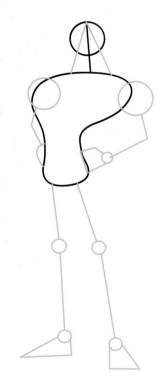

## STEP 3

Complete the arms and start to flesh out his legs. Add a mop of hair and a strong chin. Draw his belt and a line to form the bottom of his cape.

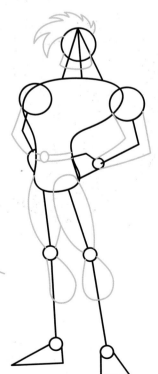

## STEP 4

Draw the rest of the cape. Add the eye mask, sloping shoulders and shins.

## STEP 5

Draw the final details before rubbing out any guide lines.

## STEP 6

We've chosen orange and green for our superhero's costume, but you can use any colours you like.

## SUPER TIP!

By choosing different colours, you can change Captain Fantastic from a hero of the day into a guardian of the night.

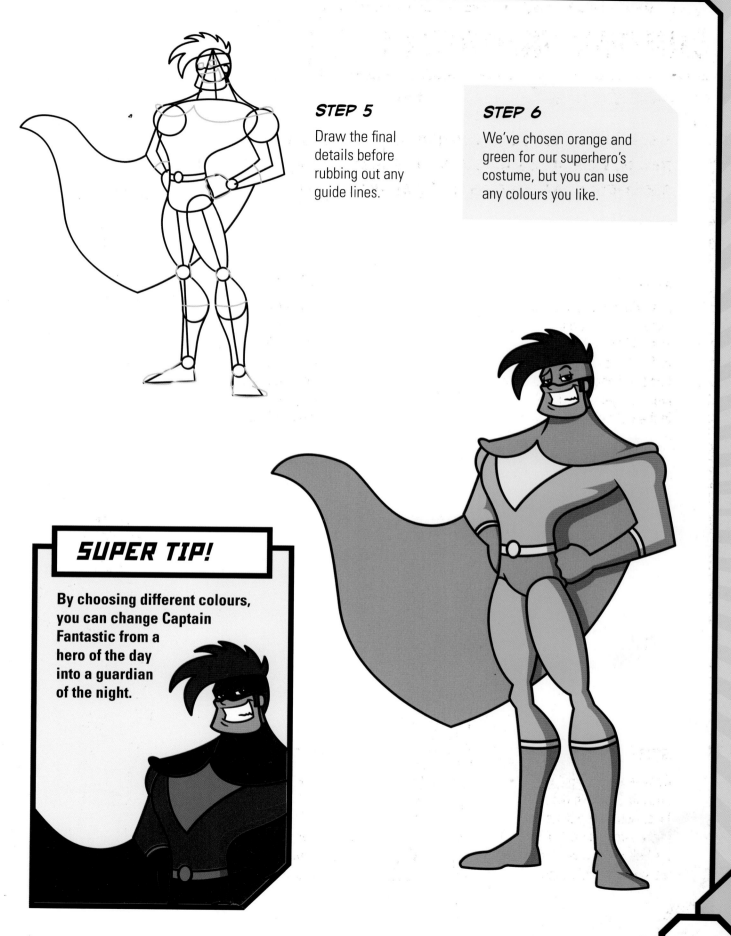

# MADAM MAYHEM

**Madam Mayhem is a villain who likes to cause chaos. She zooms along on her flying surfboard, making mischief wherever she goes.**

## STEP 1

Copy these shapes to make her body and head.

## STEP 2

Use two sausage shapes for her thighs and add a short line from her head to her body.

## STEP 3

Add her arms, lower legs and wing-like collar.

## STEP 4

Now it's time to draw her nose, spiky helmet, clenched fists and belt. Don't forget the all-important surfboard.

## STEP 5

Complete the surfboard. Draw her face and add the details to her gloves and boots. Draw a big cloud of smoke.

## STEP 6

Finally, bring your flying villain to life with spooky colours.

# THE BLUE DRAGON

The Blue Dragon looks strong and fearsome! He has sharp wings on his head and legs. Even his cape looks like a dragon's wing. Draw him if you dare!

## STEP 1

First, draw the Blue Dragon's torso and superhero underwear. Don't forget his egg-shaped head!

## STEP 2

Add his muscly arms and thighs.

## STEP 3

Draw his neck to join his head and body together. Add his lower legs and then finish his arms before adding one clenched fist.

## STEP 4

Now it's time to draw his face. Then draw a circle on his chest and add his second fist and feet. Don't forget his waistband and his gloves.

## STEP 5

Add his mask, and the
wings of his chest symbol.
The wings on his head and
legs have the same curved
edge as his cape.

## STEP 6

Use lots of different
shades of blue to colour
your Blue Dragon.

# CAPTAIN TWILIGHT

As night falls, Captain Twilight uses his magical powers to fight crime. He swoops down, wrapped in a large purple cloak.

### STEP 1

Begin by drawing Captain Twilight's head, torso and pelvis.

### STEP 2

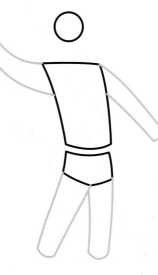

Next, draw his arms and thighs using these long, thin shapes.

### STEP 3

Draw his chin, hands and lower legs. Make the open hand big and don't join it to the wrist.

### STEP 4

Give your hero a top hat. Then draw some puffy clouds for him to stand on.

**Captain Twilight's mystical powers are easy to show by following these steps:**

- Add a wavy line around the hand, but not actually touching it.

- Add a second wavy line just outside the first.

- You could add dots and stars to make a sparkling effect.

## STEP 5

Draw his eyes and mouth, and the details of his clothes and cloak. Add some more clouds.

## STEP 6

Complete your picture by drawing a magical glow around his open hand. Then colour him in dark, mysterious colours.

# THE CRUNCHER

This metal-jawed villain is super-mean.
The Cruncher's powerful body and deadly
jaws will crush anything in sight!

### STEP 1

First, draw his
big torso and his
pelvis. Add a small
circle for his head.

### STEP 2

Then draw his
chunky arms and
thighs like this.

### STEP 3

Next, finish the
legs of his jeans and
add a belt buckle.
Draw clenched fists
before adding his
savage jaws.

### STEP 4

Now give him spiky
hair and add the
details to his clothes.

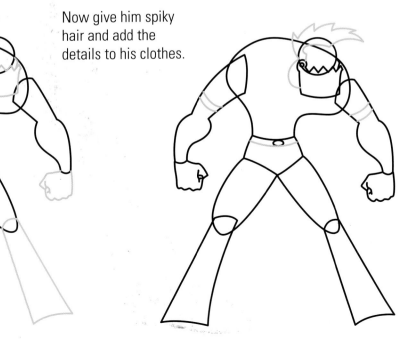

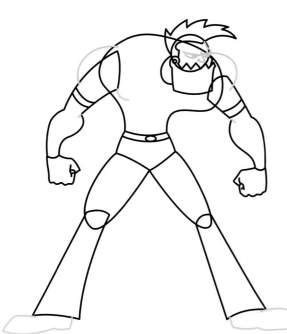

## STEP 5

Draw his face, giving him a heavy brow to make him look mean. Then, add bulging arm muscles and big feet.

## STEP 6

Now you can add colour. Use shading to show off his large chest and arm muscles.

# GALAXY GIRL

Galaxy Girl is a daring space traveller.
Armed with a cosmic wand, her mission is
to protect the world from alien attack.

### STEP 1

Begin by drawing Galaxy
Girl's head, torso and thighs.

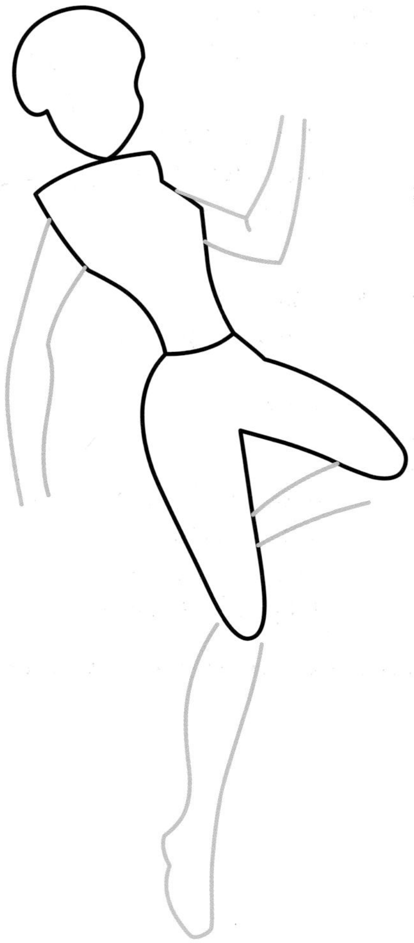

### STEP 2

Next, draw her arms and
lower legs like this, so it
looks as if she is floating
in space.

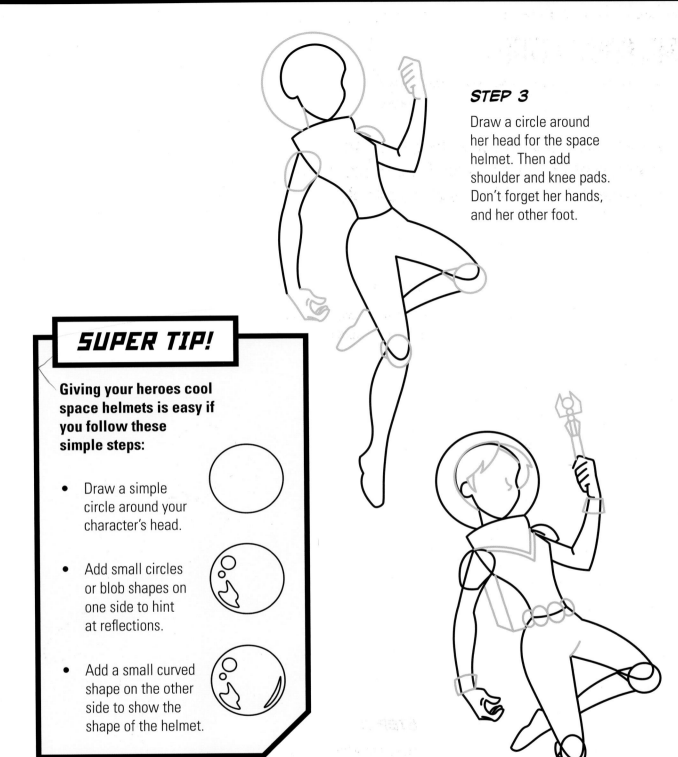

## STEP 3

Draw a circle around her head for the space helmet. Then add shoulder and knee pads. Don't forget her hands, and her other foot.

## SUPER TIP!

**Giving your heroes cool space helmets is easy if you follow these simple steps:**

- Draw a simple circle around your character's head.

- Add small circles or blob shapes on one side to hint at reflections.

- Add a small curved shape on the other side to show the shape of the helmet.

## STEP 4

Add the cosmic wand before drawing her hairline, nose and the details to her outfit. Draw an oxygen pack on her back.

## STEP 5

Draw her face and the curved breathing tube. Add oval reflection shapes to her helmet. Draw some curved lines to show the cosmic wand sending a signal.

## STEP 6

Finally, add some cool colours that will make Galaxy Girl look out of this world.

**Rocket Racer wears roller blades and a rocket backpack to blast him along at super-speed. He's so fast that bad guys don't even see him coming!**

### STEP 1

Draw a rounded shape like a balloon for his head. Add a powerful torso and superhero underwear.

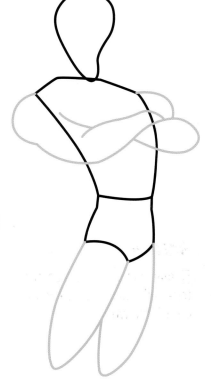

### STEP 2

Next, add his thighs and folded arms.

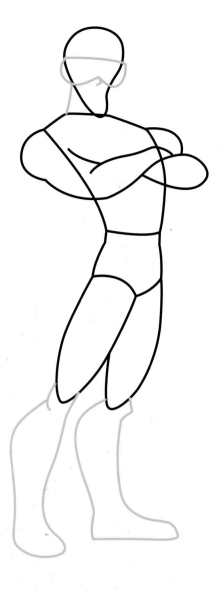

## STEP 3

Add a neck line. Then draw a large pair of cool goggles and muscly lower legs.

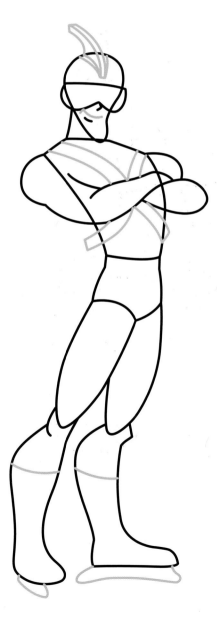

## STEP 4

Draw a helmet fin and add the straps for his backpack. Then begin to draw his roller blades.

## STEP 5

Complete his backpack and roller blades. Then add the final details to his costume.

## STEP 6

Use bright red and yellow details to bring your hero to life.

# GLOSSARY

**brow** Forehead.

**character** A person in a picture or story.

**compass** An instrument for drawing circles.

**HB** A pencil with a lead that is neither hard nor soft, but somewhere in between.

**laboratory** A place where scientists do experiments.

**mystical** Mysterious and fascinating.

**pelvis** The bony frame at the base of the spine to which the legs are attached.

**poster paint** A water-based, bright-coloured paint often used for posters.

**torso** The trunk of the human body – from the neck to the pelvis.

**vertical** Up and down (rather than sideways).

**watercolour** An artist's paint that is thinned with water to give it a transparent quality.

# FURTHER READING

*The Super Book for Superheroes* by Jason Ford (Laurence King, 2013)

*Superheroes* by Ted Rechlin (Dover Children's, 2012)

*What to Doodle? Robots and Superheroes* by Peter Donahue (Dover Children's, 2013)

# WEBSITES

www.hellokids.com/r_484/coloring-pages/super-heroes-coloring-pages

www.how-to-draw-cartoons-online.com

www.my-how-to-draw.com

# INDEX